The Omaha

T 20151

Madelyn Klein Anderson

Watts LIBRARY

Franklin Watts
A Division of Grolier Publishing
New York • London • Hong Kong • Sydney
Danbury, Connecticut

Note to readers: Definitions for words in **bold** can be found in the Glossary at the back of this book.

Photographs ©: Archive Photos: 6; Art Resource, NY: 3 top, 36 (National Museum of American Art, Washington, DC.); Corbis-Bettmann: 41 (UPI), 18 left, 42; Edith Tarbescu: 26; From the Collection of Deborah Goodsite: 35 (The Century Magazine, January 1894, #3); Joslyn Art Museum, Omaha, NE.: 3 bottom, 29 (*Mandan Shrine* by Karl Bodmer), 9 top (NA69/*Buffalo and Elk on the Upper Missouri River* by Karl Bodmer, watercolor), 27 (*Omaha boy* by Karl Bodmer, watercolor on paper/Gift of Enron Art Foundation/Photo by Malcolm Varon); Lincoln Journal: 12 (Betty Stevens); Nebraska State Historical Society: 10, 16, 24, 33, 43 bottom; New England Stock Photo: 14 (L. O'Shaughnessy); North Wind Picture Archives: 9 bottom, 17, 19, 20, 21, 23, 43 top; Omaha World-Herald: 4 (Bill Batson); Peter Arnold Inc.: 44 (Ed Reschke); Reinhard Brucker: 22, 45; Rudy Smith: 18 right, 46, 49, 50, 52, 53; Smithsonian Institution, Washington, DC: 31 (3987), 11 (Anthropological Archives, #47,702B); Stock Montage, Inc.: 7, 32, 38, 40.

Cover illustration by Gary Overacre, interpreted from a photograph by © Corbis-Bettmann.

Map by XNR Productions Inc.

Visit Franklin Watts on the Internet at:
http://publishing.grolier.com

Library of Congress Cataloging-in-Publication Data

Anderson, Madelyn Klein.
    The Omaha / Madelyn Klein Anderson.
        p.   cm.— (Watts Library)
    Includes bibliographical references and index.
    Summary: Examines the culture of the Omaha Indians, from their life in North America before the Europeans' arrival to the present day.
    ISBN: 0-531-20404-9 (lib. bdg.)   0-531-16481-0 (pbk.)
    1. Omaha Indians Juvenile literature. [1. Omaha Indians. 2. Indians of North America.] I. Title. II. Series.
E99.O4A53   2000
978'.004975—dc21

99-29816
CIP

Contents

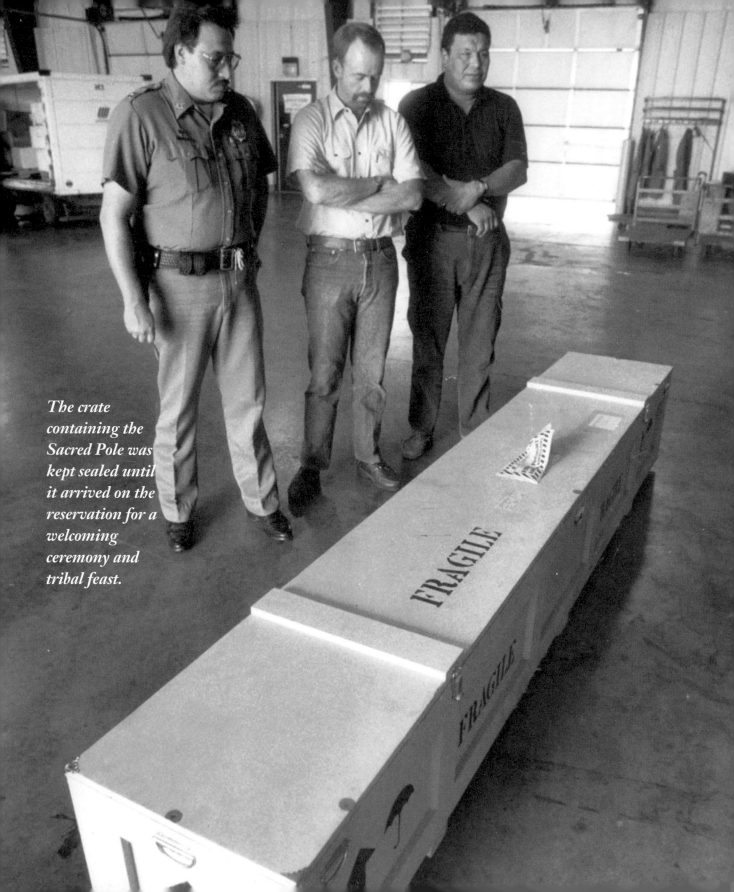

The crate containing the Sacred Pole was kept sealed until it arrived on the reservation for a welcoming ceremony and tribal feast.

FRAGILE

Chapter One

The Sacred Pole Returns

On July 12, 1989, the waiting room of the Eppley Airfield in Eppley, Nebraska, was crowded. The air hummed with anticipation. The Sacred Pole of the Omaha Indians, the symbol of Omaha power and unity, was coming home after more than one hundred years. The plane touched down, and soon the 8-foot (2-meter)-long Sacred Pole, with its tightly bound medicine bag and plumed crest, was in the eager hands of the Omaha. A motorcade escorted the pole past the cheering

The Pole Today

The Sacred Pole is currently on display in a Nebraska museum. It is also known to the Omaha as the "Venerable Man." (*Venerable* is another word for sacred.)

people of all races who lined the highway to the Omaha reservation in Macy, Nebraska. There, the Sacred Pole was received with solemn **rites**, to be temporarily stored at the University of Nebraska until the Omaha could provide it with an appropriate setting.

The date of the Sacred Pole's return was chosen deliberately. More than two hundred years ago, on July 12, 1775, the Second Continental Congress assumed control over all Indian tribes in what was to become the United States of America. This action set the stage for a hundred years of fighting and heartbreak that ended the Indian way of life. No matter how hard the Indians fought the Americans—or tried to coexist with them as the Omaha did—the hordes of immigrants pour-

The Second Continental Congress

ing into their lands had the protection of the United States government and could not be withstood.

Most researchers believe that the so-called **indigenous**, or native, people of North America—often called Indians and Eskimos—were once immigrants themselves. They were nomadic hunters who followed mammoths and giant sloths across the frozen Bering Strait between Asia and North

A prehistoric hunting expedition

Many Members, One Language

Although spread out across the continent, the Omaha were united by an ancient language called Siouan.

America during the Ice Age. They gradually fanned out over the North American continent as far east as Greenland, where they probably drove out the white settlers, in an **erratic** course of twists and turns that took thousands of years. A tribe might move south then turn north, or move east and then turn west. The Omaha, which included groups from the Carolinas, Georgia, and the Dakotas, seem to have gone west and possibly north. They lived with many other tribes on their centuries-long trek, such as the Sioux, the northern Cheyenne, and the Osage, and they shared skills and customs. As the Omaha moved, bands sometimes lost track of one another at river crossings or in storms, and they were rarely reunited. As a result, their numbers decreased, and the risk of **assimilation** or destruction by larger tribes increased. The Omaha came to realize that they had settle in one place and grow strong if they were to survive.

When the Omaha reached the Missouri River, they found a land that pleased them—the grasslands of the southern Great Plains. Buffalo, their source of food, clothing, and shelter, were plentiful. On the far side of the river there were fields of maize, or Indian corn, and the sturdy sod houses of the Arikara. The Omaha drove out the Arikara and took over their land. Thus the Omaha became farmers who had some control over their food supply, as well as hunters and gatherers. They were able to stay in one place and set up an orderly, stable way of life. Their new lifestyle led to many rules, regulations, and rituals, and each of the tribe's numerous clans, or family

Ethnologists

Ethnologists are scientists who study races of people, their origins, and characteristics.

8

Elk and buffalo wade in the Upper Missouri River.

The Omaha made houses, called earth lodges, using mounds of dirt and other materials.

Francis LaFlesche, left, and his wife Susette, around 1890.

groups, had its place and its function. This social order lasted for centuries, until the arrival of the new immigrants.

The Omaha had no written language, so everything we know about them comes mainly from the efforts of two 19th-century ethnologists who recorded Omaha history. Alice Fletcher of the Peabody Museum in Cambridge, Massachusetts, lived among the Omaha for many years. Her assistant, Francis LaFlesche, was the son of an Omaha chief and the grandson of a French fur trapper. In order to preserve their history, the Omaha cooperated with these two scientists. A third researcher, Dr. John Comfort Fillmore, worked separately to **transcribe** Omaha music into European form. Fletcher and LaFlesche were responsible for saving the Sacred Pole after the tribal structure broke down.

As the Omaha and other Indian tribes learned to exert political pressure and increasingly demanded their civil rights, they requested the return of their sacred objects from the Peabody, particularly the Sacred Pole. Under the Native American Grave Protection and Repatriation Act of 1990, which calls for the return of sacred objects when requested by the tribe to which they originally belonged, these items were returned to the Omaha. Some blame has been placed on Alice Fletcher, as a non-Indian, for convincing the Omaha to send these **relics** away. But if they had not been sent away, the Sacred Pole and other **artifacts** would probably have disappeared forever.

Without Alice Fletcher and Francis LaFlesche, we would not have much firsthand knowledge of the Omaha and their traditional way of life. The two researchers had countless interviews with Omaha men and women, and made their observations over many years. The knowledge we have, like all knowledge

Preserving the Pole

The last keeper of the Sacred Pole was an elderly Omaha man named Yellow Smoke. In 1883, he posed for this photograph while representing the Indian people at an exposition in Amsterdam, Holland. Yellow Smoke had planned to have the pole buried with him when he died, because his descendants did not want to take responsibility for it while they were struggling to survive in a new culture. Instead, Fletcher and LaFlesche sent the pole and other Omaha objects to the Peabody Museum of Archaeology and Ethnology at Harvard University in Cambridge, Massachusetts, for preservation.

The Omaha Tribal Chairman blesses the Sacred Buffalo Hide after its return to the tribe in 1991.

gained from oral history, has its confusions and gaps. Oral history is retold many times before it is written down. However, it is a history of which the Omaha people are proud.

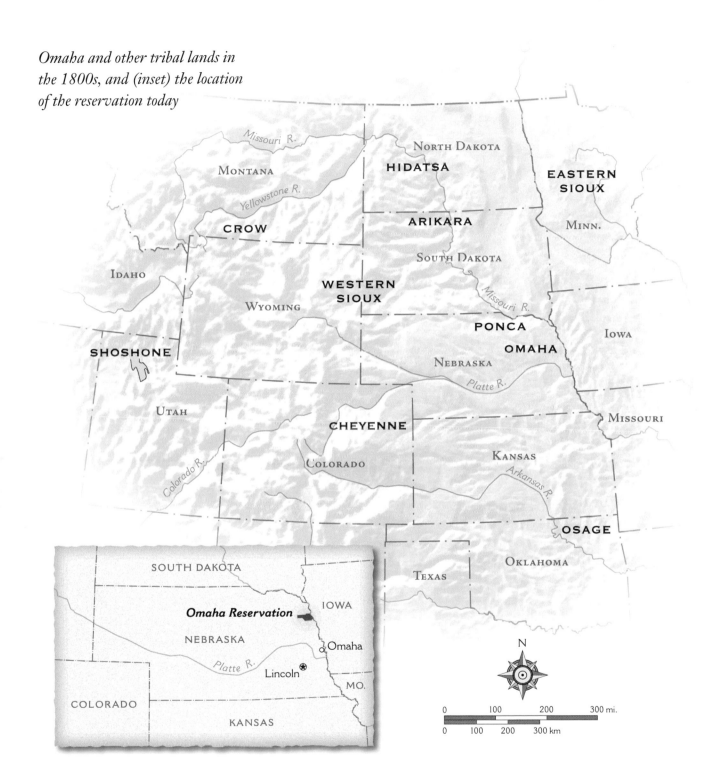

Omaha and other tribal lands in the 1800s, and (inset) the location of the reservation today

MONTANA

Missouri R.

Yellowstone R.

NORTH DAKOTA

HIDATSA

EASTERN SIOUX

ARIKARA

MINN.

SOUTH DAKOTA

CROW

IDAHO

WESTERN SIOUX

WYOMING

Missouri R.

PONCA

OMAHA

IOWA

SHOSHONE

NEBRASKA

Platte R.

UTAH

MISSOURI

CHEYENNE

COLORADO

Colorado R.

KANSAS

Arkansas R.

OSAGE

OKLAHOMA

TEXAS

SOUTH DAKOTA

IOWA

Omaha Reservation

NEBRASKA

Omaha

Platte R.

Lincoln ⊛

MO.

COLORADO

KANSAS

N

0   100   200   300 mi.

0   100   200   300 km

13

Creation stories tell of the Earth's gifts of fire, tools, and animals to the Omaha people.

Chapter Two

The Sacred Legend

The Omaha Sacred Legend, passed down from generation to generation, told of Omaha beginnings.

In the beginning, the people were in water. They opened their eyes but they could see nothing. As the people came out of the water, they were naked. But after many days passed they desired covering. They took the fiber of weeds and grass and wove it together for clothing. After this, the people built grass houses. They cut the grass with the shoulder blade of a deer.

A fire-making ceremony at an Omaha powwow

The people lived near a large body of water in a wooded country where there were animals. The men hunted the deer with clubs. They did not know the use of the bow and arrow. The people wandered about the shores of the great water and were poor and cold. And the people thought, "What will we do to help ourselves?" They found a bluish stone that was easily flaked and chipped and they made knives and arrowheads out of it.

They now had knives and arrows, but they suffered from the cold and the people thought, "What will we do?" A man found a dry elm

16

root and dug a hole in it and put a stick in and rubbed it. Then smoke came. At last a spark came. It was blown into a flame and fire came to warm the people and to cook their food.

Now the people had fire and ate their meat roasted, but they tired of roasted meat. A man found a bunch of clay that stuck well together. Then he brought sand to mix with it and he molded it as a vessel. Then he gathered grass and made a heap. He put the clay vessel in the grass, set it on fire, and made the clay vessel hard. He put water into the vessel with meat and put the vessel over the fire. The people had boiled meat to eat.

Then a man found some blue, red, and white kernels. He thought he had found something of great value, so he hid them in a mound. One day he went to see if they were safe. When he came to the mound he found it covered with stalks that had ears bearing kernels of these colors. He took an ear of each kind and gave the rest to the people. They tried it for food, found it good, and built mounds like the first and buried the corn in them. So the corn grew and the people had abundant food.

It was difficult to gather and keep the people's grass coverings. The people thought, "What can we do to have something different to wear?" Before this, they had been throwing away the hides they had taken from the game. So they used their stone knives to scrape the hides and use them for clothing.

Then the grass houses became unsatisfactory and the people thought, "How will we better ourselves?"

One of the first gifts Indians gave to colonial settlers was maize, or corn.

These Indians are scraping a buffalo hide.

So they substituted bark for grass as a covering for their dwellings. But they were determined to put skins on the poles of their dwellings. They tried the deerskins, but they were too small. They tried the elk, but both deer and elk skins became hard and unmanageable under the sun and the rain. Until they had the buffalo, the people could not have good tents. Then when they did, the buffalo skin made comfortable tent covers.

18

Dogs were fitted with packs and travois to help move nomadic peoples from place to place.

The Sacred Legend also told of important developments:

The people wandered into the forests where the birch trees grow and where there were great lakes. They made birch-bark canoes and traveled in them. A man discovered two young animals and carried them home. He fed them and they grew large and were docile. He discovered that these animals (dogs) would carry loads, so a harness was fixed on them to which poles were fastened and they became beasts of burden.

Docile

Docile means "calm and easy to manage or train."

19

Indians used horses to hunt and to travel great distances across the Plains.

Then another man discovered two animals. Fearing them, he tried to get away, but the animals stayed near him. When they reached the village, the people were curious. The people found the animals could carry loads and be led by a string. There were two, male and female. They multiplied and this is the way horses came to the Omaha. The people loved the horses, so dogs were no longer the only beasts of burden.

The Sacred Legend offers no spirits or magic, as do some other tribes' creation stories. Instead, the legend speaks about the **ingenuity** of the Omaha.

The organization of a governing council is described briefly in the Sacred Legend: "The people said, 'Let us appoint men who shall preserve order.' Accordingly, they selected the wisest, the most thoughtful, generous, and kind men, and they consulted together and agreed upon a council of seven who should govern the people."

Two Pipes

The pipe of the Sky People was masculine. The pipe of the Earth People was feminine. In ceremonies, the two pipes were always brought together.

Although religion is not mentioned in the Sacred Legend, the rigid Omaha tribal organization was based on religious ideas. The Omaha believed that an invisible force activated all movement, including the actions of people and nature. It was certain that night would follow day, that winter would follow summer, that mountains would stand, and that rivers would flow. All things were related through this life force.

The Omaha regarded nature as either male or female. The sky and the sun were father, the earth was mother, and the union of the two produced human beings. To reinforce this belief, the tribe was divided into Sky People and Earth People. Each division had a principal chief and a tribal pipe.

The Sky People and the Earth People were each divided into five groups. These groups, called clans, were extended families related through the father. Their leadership was **hereditary**—it passed from father to son. Each clan had its

A museum display shows an Omaha tent for sacred pipes.

Spring Thunder

The first thunder of spring was an important event to the Omaha. It marked the awakening of Earth's life-giving force after its winter sleep.

own ceremonies in addition to those of the entire tribe, and its own **taboos**. For example, the Elk clan could not hunt or eat the meat of the elk. Each clan also had a set of names it could give to children in infancy and another set for when they grew older.

The five clans of the Sky People lived in the southern half of the village, which was laid out in a circle. They also sat on the southern half of the tribal circle during meetings and ceremonies. The Sky People were in charge of the Omaha's physical welfare. One clan of the Sky People controlled the Sacred Tent of War and the ceremonies connected with the first thunder of spring. The other four clans of the Sky People were in charge of the ceremonies associated with food. One of these four clans was also in charge of the other two sacred tents— one holding the Sacred Pole, and one holding the Sacred White Buffalo Hide. The keeper of the Sacred White Buffalo Hide conducted the rites for the buffalo hunt and for the planting of maize. The keeper of the Sacred Pole conducted the rites for preserving the authority of the tribe's governing council and for power and good fortune in war and hunting.

The five clans of the Earth People lived in the northern part of the village and sat on the northern half of the tribal circle. These clans were in charge of rites relating to creation, the stars, and the cosmic forces behind all life. Most of these rites were less practical than those of the Sky People and had faded from memory by the time Omaha history was recorded.

The three sacred tents of the Omaha tribal circle, or Hoo-Thu-Ga

An Omaha woman with her child on a cradle board, around 1920

Chapter Three

The Four Hills

The Omaha believed that life was a journey over four hills. "Reaching the Fourth Hill" meant having a long and successful life. The First Hill was infancy. Every child was given moccasins with a little hole in the sole. If a spirit came to take the infant away, the child could point to the "worn-out" moccasins that prevented any journey. Four days after birth, each child was given a baby name. On the eighth day, the tribal priest stood at the entrance to the infant's home and announced the birth to all the elements of earth and sky, and all the animals, plants, and bodies of water. They were

Baby Gifts

Omaha baby boys were given a belt decorated with the claws of a wildcat. Baby girls received a belt made of mussel shells.

asked to watch over the child as he or she traveled over the difficult road of life.

The Second Hill was childhood. It was marked by a ceremony called "Turning the Child," which was held in spring, after the first thunder. A tent was set up and made sacred, the keeper of the rites got ready, and the tribal **herald** walked through the village calling to parents whose children were old enough to walk by themselves. The children were brought to the tent, each carrying a new pair of moccasins—without holes—to show that he or she was prepared for the long journey of life. A fire was lit in the center of the tent. Then, a rock

Beaded moccasins

was placed to the east of the fire, and a ball of grass to the west. The mother brought the child to the opening of the tent, presented the keeper with many gifts, and the child walked into the tent alone. There, the keeper told how the gifts would bring the child a future filled with many good things in a life that would "reach the fourth hill."

The keeper sang a ritual song to the four winds as he lifted the child by the shoulders and rested the child's feet on the stone—first facing east, then south, then north, and west. The slightest misstep meant disaster, because turning in the direction of the winds symbolized the child's ability to overcome the problems and sorrows of life. Then the child put on the new moccasins and took four steps, one for each hill. Afterward, the keeper called out to the world that the child's baby name was being thrown away, and a new name was announced. The child was then told about the taboos that had to be observed as a member of the clan and what the penalty would be for disobedience. This ended the ritual for a girl child, who then returned to her mother. For a boy—a future warrior—there was one more step in this ceremony.

This painting of an Omaha boy shows the tuft of hair and the circular pattern of his clan on the crown of his head.

A tuft of the boy's hair was cut off and put into a small pouch. This consecrated the boy to the god of thunder, the power that controlled the life or death of a warrior. Members of the clan in charge of thunder rites, who were camped at the entrance to the tent during the rituals, met the boy when he came out. The clan then turned the boy over to his father, who took him home and cut his hair once again, this time in the symbolic pattern prescribed for each clan. The hair was kept in this pattern until the boy had all his second teeth. Then the hair was allowed to grow in until a circle of hair on the crown of his head could be braided into a scalp lock. This was the sign of reaching the Third Hill, which was adulthood. Honors won in battle were worn on this lock of hair. If a warrior was killed in battle, the scalp lock might become an enemy's **trophy**.

The entrance into adulthood required that all boys—and any girls who wanted to— undergo a rite of fasting, isolation, and prayer. This was common among Plains Indian tribes

A Sacred Rite

The Sacred Legend describes the Omaha rite of puberty: There was a time when the people felt themselves weak and poor. The old men decided when the children were ready to go to the hills for four days, their heads covered with clay, to pray and cry. "When they stop, they shall wipe their tears with the palms of their hands and lift their wet hands to the sky, then lay them on the earth." While praying, they were forbidden to ask for favors from the Great Mysterious Power, but to accept whatever was offered.

This Indian prays in isolation at a holy site.

such as the Sioux, the Blackfoot, the Comanche, and the Kiowa, and took place at **puberty**.

The young person seeking a vision entered adulthood, the Third Hill, whether or not a vision was granted. But visions were common after four days without food or water,

Gift-Giving

Gift-giving was important among the Omaha, not only to become a member of a society or to obtain favors, but to gain honor. Those who gained honor as gift-givers and good hunters became chiefs.

Woman Songs

Omaha men also sang what were known as "woman songs," but these were never sung to a woman. They were songs about unhappy marriages or aggressive young women, and were considered disrespectful.

particularly for young men to whom they mattered a great deal. Some visions were considered luckier than others: hawks were good, snakes were bad, and a vision of the moon meant disaster. To ignore these visions was to invite tragedy. The vision came with a call or song to be remembered in times of need for as long as life lasted. The young person was forbidden to speak of his vision except to an elder who had experienced a similar vision. Societies of people with similar visions were an important part of Omaha life, but many gifts had to be offered before a young man could become a member of such a society.

Friendships, often begun in childhood, were highly valued among Omaha men and women. Friends were part of every event in each other's life. Male friends would paint each other's faces for war and for courting young women, an important ritual of adulthood. Young men were forbidden to visit young women in their homes, so contact had to be made at social gatherings. For example, when a young woman went to get the family's supply of water, a would-be suitor would often hide nearby in the grass and play a love song on his flute.

Marriages could take place only between members of different clans whose mothers had no close blood relationship. Some marriages were arranged, but others were between couples whose parents consented to the union. The courting ritual was very specific. After playing a few songs on the flute and speaking a few words in passing, the young man praised the girl and her family publicly, and asked her parents for the favor

of her hand. Marriage was usually by **elopement** to one of the
young man's relatives. Gifts were then exchanged between the
families. Should the parents on either side object at any time,
the marriage was still valid, but the new couple would find life
difficult.

Polygamy—having more than one wife at a time—was allowed, usually because one wife could not do all the work that was required of her. A wife sewed the family's clothing, tended the maize, gathered berries and roots, fished, collected wood for the family fire, and cooked all the food. When the village followed the buffalo, she put up the tent, took it down again, and carried it along with the household goods. She also carried the young children and whatever else the dogs or horses could not carry. Under these circumstances it is no

Omaha wives do chores outside the earth lodge they share.

wonder that women were willing to accept another wife in the family. Some tribes took prisoners on raids and used them as slaves to do all these chores, but the Omaha did not take prisoners. Neither did they allow themselves to be taken prisoner, preferring to die instead. It is probable that there was a **surplus** of Omaha women who would rather be a second or third wife than have no husband to hunt for her food.

The Omaha preferred peace and order, so they put many restrictions on waging a war, unless it was a defensive one. Permission to go to war had to be given by the Council of Seven. Anyone defying the council would be sent naked into the Sacred Tent of War. There, the council had a staff, or long stick, with a splintered end to which rattlesnake poison could be applied. A sudden prod with the staff would send the deadly venom through the rebel's veins. But if the council wanted to warn rather than kill the person, the staff would be used on his horses.

Defensive warfare, however, was thought to preserve the honor of the tribe. Rites performed with the Sacred Pole and the Sacred War Pack were supposed to bring good fortune in war. If a warrior returned victorious, he wore his war honors on his scalp lock and his chest was tattooed with a mark of honor.

Tattoos of honor mark this Omaha woman.

33

His daughters could also be tattooed, which greatly increased their value as wives.

Respect, honor, and a rest from the difficulties of life were the rewards of reaching the Fourth, and last, Hill. After crossing that hill into death, there was a journey along the Milky Way of stars. Here, there was an old man wrapped in a buffalo cloak who looked for the clan taboo sign and guided each good person toward his or her relatives. Murderers, virtually the only evil people the Omaha recognized, were condemned to wander the Milky Way endlessly, whistling as they went. No wonder Omaha children were frightened by the sound of whistling!

The funeral song was cheerful, meant to comfort the dead on their journey along the starry road. The dead person's belong-

Legend of Blackbird's Burial

A story from the journals of Lewis and Clark, the explorers who mapped the Louisiana Purchase from 1804 to 1806, tells of Blackbird, an Omaha chief, who was buried sitting on his still-living horse. The Omaha denied this story, adding that Blackbird was despised for gaining power by poisoning his rivals, and horses were too well loved to bury them alive.

ings were distributed among friends or given to the winner of a foot race. If a young man died, his favorite horse might be killed to accompany him on his journey. Death brought great mourning. Even years later, someone thinking of a dead loved one might start wailing, and the wailing was soon echoed by others around the camp.

Omaha men sing the death song, their arms and shoulder blades hung with willow branches.

35

A portrait of Big Elk, 1832

Chapter Four

The Flood

My chiefs, braves, and young men, I have just returned from a visit to a far-off country toward the rising sun [Washington, D.C.] *and have seen many strange things. I bring to you news which it saddens my heart to think of. There is a coming flood which will reach us, and I advise you to prepare for it. Soon the animals which* [the Mysterious Spirit] *has given us for* **sustenance** *will disappear beneath this flood to return no more, and it will be very hard for you. Look at me. You see I am advanced in age. I can no longer think for you and lead you as in my younger days. You must think for yourselves what will be best for your welfare. I tell you this that* *you may be prepared for the coming change. You may not know my meaning. Many of you are old, as I am, and by the time that change comes we may be lying peacefully in our graves, but these young men will remain to suffer. Speak kindly to one another. Do what you can to help each other, even in the troubles with the coming tide. Now, my people, this is all I have to say. Bear these words in mind, and when the time comes think of what I have said.*

These are the words of Big Elk, a great Omaha chief. They were spoken in 1853, after he returned from treaty discussions in Washington, D.C. He knew that the Omaha way of life could not survive the flood of different people and their ways. For thirty-eight years, the Omaha had signed treaties

Omaha horsemen in pursuit, led by a runner carrying the Sacred Pole

Smallpox

Smallpox is a disease caused by a virus that travels from person to person through the air. A vaccine now exists to prevent smallpox, but the disease was once a serious threat, often resulting in death. Smallpox was brought to America by the Europeans, and American Indians had no natural resistance to it. As a result, many Indians died.

acknowledging the U.S. government's **supremacy** over them and had sold their claims to land in what is now Missouri and Iowa. The Omaha were also under frequent attack by the Sioux, who tried to take their horses in order to gain power to fight the newcomers. The Omaha moved their villages from the Missouri River to get away from the Sioux. They chose to move closer to the U. S. Indian Agency, and thus gave up their independence in exchange for protection. This move also enabled the agency to **wield** more power in supervising the tribes in this area. One result that benefited the Omaha was their decision to allow the government to **vaccinate** them against smallpox. As a result, the Omaha avoided the terrible loss of life that other tribes suffered in epidemics of that deadly disease.

As Big Elk predicted, the flood of change overwhelming the Omaha was only the beginning. Just after Big Elk's death in 1853, the Omaha handed over all but 300,000 acres (121,400 hectares) of their hunting grounds along the Missouri River to the government. The payments for this land were to be made over forty years. Also, the Omaha were to be

An Omaha buffalo hunter steadies his bow.

given a sawmill, a gristmill, and the services of a blacksmith and farmer to help them become an agricultural society. A section of reservation land was to be surveyed for homes for those who wanted them. Another treaty, in 1865, sold off the northern part of the Omaha reservation for the use of the Winnebago tribe, whom the government was moving from Minnesota. The Omaha needed to buy some of the tools and household goods the traders and settlers used, but part of the payment they received was in the form of livestock and farming tools.

After that there were no more treaties. The U.S. government decided that all agreements with the tribes would be made by act of Congress with the consent of the tribe. The Omaha were involved with several such acts of Congress. They sold 50,000 acres (20,200 ha) from the western part of the reservation—again in order to buy livestock, farming equipment, and houses. They also wanted to build schools. Another act sold yet more land to the Winnebago. In an act passed in August 1882, each Omaha man, woman, and child was given a piece of reservation land that was not to be sold or taxed for twenty-five years. Land in the southwest of

A group of Omaha "allotted Indians" on reservation land

the reservation that was not set aside for the tribe was made available for sale.

Then a new problem arose. The Ponca, who may have once been part of the Omaha tribe, were forcibly removed to Oklahoma Territory. Despite their **allotted** land, the Omaha feared that they might also be sent away. After an investigation, they found to their despair that they did not have written deeds to their individual holdings. Alice Fletcher, the Peabody Museum ethnologist working among the Omaha, came to the rescue. She went to Washington, D.C., where she **lobbied** for

The Ponca, a tribe closely related to the Omaha, gather to perform the Sun Dance.

years in the halls of Congress and cornered influential people at social gatherings. Finally, in 1887, an act of Congress provided written guarantees of the Omaha land allotments. And as "allotted Indians," the Omaha were also made citizens of the United States.

In 1894, a railroad was built through the reservation. The twenty-five-year prohibition on sales of allotted property expired just as the railroad was completed in 1907, and much land was sold. Soon, two towns sprang up along the railroad tracks. Some Omaha returned to live in three traditional villages on reservation land. Others chose to live in town. Scorned as "make-believe white men" by their reservation brothers, the town Omaha built businesses and schools.

Settlers arrived and towns were founded as the Union Pacific railroad was built across Nebraska.

An Omaha family shops at the country store in Macy, Nebraska, 1923.

Buffalo

Huge herds of buffalo once roamed the Great Plains of North America. They were the primary source of food, clothing, and shelter for the Plains Indians, including the Omaha. During the late 1800s, American hunters almost completely wiped out the buffalo herds. As a result, the Indians lost a vital part of their way of life.

They needed money to buy household goods, fabrics, and food, so they took jobs, prepared themselves for professions, and earned money to buy instead of barter.

The reservation Omaha found life more difficult. The buffalo that had provided their food, clothing, and shelter for centuries were disappearing. Hunters had killed too many animals for the herds to recover. What had happened to the promise of the Great Spirit to provide the people with buffalo forever? The Omaha were bewildered, and their faith was challenged. Their self-sufficient way of life was gone. The Omaha had to turn to farming and selling their surplus crops in the town. They changed their way of life almost as much as their town brothers had. Clans broke down, traditions were forgotten, and young men did not want the responsibility of caring for the Sacred Pole or the Sacred White Buffalo Hide. These things were no longer important in daily life. The old men had their relics buried with them to

keep them from being thrown away like garbage. The flood of change that Big Elk had spoken of had finally overcome the Omaha.

A sewing kit made by Omaha Indians from a buffalo bladder

The Omaha Nation occupies reservation land in Macy, Nebraska.

Welcome to Macy

The Omaha People

The First People of Nebraska

Chapter Five

Struggling to Survive

The Omaha were not the only people who lost their traditional way of life. The immigrants who came to this new land and displaced the Omaha also lost many of their customs and beliefs. Since the beginning of time, cultures have changed and people have had to adapt to those changes. Today, instead of just accepting what they are given, as in the days of chiefs such as Big Elk, the Omaha use politics to get what they want. The head of tribal government is now called a chairman, and the Omaha are the Omaha Nation. The Sacred Pole is a symbol not only of the ancient ways but also of the political power of the Omaha Nation that **negotiated** its return. No longer do the Omaha need an Alice Fletcher to speak for them in Congress: they have their own lawyers and other professionals now.

The Omaha Nation has been using its sovereign status to try to improve the economic well-being of its 6,000 members, particularly the 3,400 who live on the reservation. At the end of the twentieth century, the Omaha unemployment rate was about 60 percent, approximately twelve times the national rate. The Omaha have tried to generate more income by using their sovereign-state advantage to offer legal gambling on the reservation. They built a gambling casino on a part of the reservation that crosses the Missouri River and juts into the state of Iowa. But riverboat gambling on the Missouri is also legal, and the competition has prevented the casino from being the successful source of revenue the Omaha had hoped for. In 1997, they turned to a more **controversial** source of income and jobs—the manufacture of cigarettes.

The Omaha Nation Tobacco Company buys tobacco from North Carolina and makes cigarettes in a small factory in

Macy, Nebraska. They use older machines that require more employees to operate them. This may not be an efficient way to compete with America's huge tobacco companies, but there are some advantages. A pack of Omaha Full-Flavor cigarettes costs about half as much as a pack of well-known brands, and sales on reservations around the country are rising rapidly. The company is lobbying for exemption from state and federal laws that try to discourage smoking by demanding huge price

The front entrance of Casino Omaha, left, and the colorful sign that beckons tourists, right

increases and stiff bans on how cigarettes can be marketed. The Omaha are also trying to get exemption from paying damages for smoking-related diseases that occurred before their company was formed. If these exemptions are allowed, the Omaha Nation Tobacco Company would be even more competitive.

To compete with other brands, Omaha cigarettes are sold for as little as $1.00 a pack.

At the same time, the Omaha Nation, like other Indian tribes, may also bring a lawsuit against the large tobacco companies for having caused smoking-related diseases among its members. This seems **illogical** in a tribe now hoping to profit from cigarettes, but the Omaha seem to see the issue as historical. The **compensation** they seek is for diseases that have already developed, and afflicted Omaha people should be compensated. And if Indians smoke more than the rest of the U.S. population, why shouldn't an Indian company profit from their habit? Their position is that life expectancy among Indians is lower and the suicide rate is higher than among other groups of Americans. So most Indians do not live long enough to die from the smoking-related diseases that often kill older people. But the lack of job skills and money is devastating, so they feel that earning money by making cigarettes is more important than the effects of smoking. This may not sound like a "socially acceptable" position, but it is the view of a people struggling to survive—and manufacturing cigarettes is still legal.

Omaha leaders may find other socially acceptable opportunities for reducing unemployment and increasing income. For example, the exhibition of historical objects such as the Sacred Pole may make tourism more profitable. Meanwhile, the people of the Omaha Nation are determined to survive—and prosper—as best they can.

Homes on the Omaha reservation, with cornfields in the foreground

Glossary

allotted—given out in equal parts

artifacts—objects used by humans in the past

assimilation—adopting the culture of a group

compensation—making up for something

controversial—causing a difference of opinion

elopement—running away to get married

erratic—irregular

herald—an official messenger

heredity—the passing of traits from parents to children

illogical—something that does not make sense

indigenous—occurring naturally in a region

ingenuity—the quality of being inventive

lobbied—tried to get politicians to vote in a certain way

negotiated—tried to reach an agreement

puberty—the time when a child is changing into an adult

relics—things that have survived from the past

rite—a ceremonial act

supremacy—the highest power

surplus—more than is needed

sustenance—support; the necessities of life

taboos—prohibitions; actions that are not allowed

transcribe—to make a written copy of

trophy—a prize or award

vaccinate—to give an injection that prevents against disease

wield—to handle

To Find Out More

Books

Ferris, Jeri. *Native American Doctor: The Story of Susan LaFlesche Picotte*. Minneapolis, MN: Lerner, 1991.

Freedman, Russell (Illus. by Karl Bodmer). *Indian Winter*. New York: Holiday House, 1992.

LaFlesche, Francis. *The Middle Five: Indian Schoolboys of the Omaha Tribe*. Lincoln, NE: University of Nebraska Press (Bison Books), 1978.

Marsh, Carole. *Nebraska Timeline: A Chronology of Nebraska History, Mystery, Trivia, Legend, Lore, and More*. Peachtree City, GA: Gallopede, 1994.

Native Americans of the Northwest (Indians of North America series). Broomall, PA: Chelsea House, 1990.

Ridington, Robin and Dennis Hastings. *Blessing for a Long Time: The Sacred Pole of the Omaha Tribe*. Lincoln, NE: University of Nebraska Press, 1997.

Welsch, Roger L. *Omaha Tribal Myths and Trickster Tales*. Lincoln, NE: J and L Lee Co., 1994

Videos

Dancing to Give Thanks
(Vision Maker, Lincoln, NE, 1988, 30 minutes) Documents the annual powwow, and celebrates the traditions and family customs of the Omaha. The film includes numerous interviews and examples of fancy dancing.

The Return of the Sacred Pole
(Nebraska Public Television, 1992, 28 minutes) Tells the story of how "The Venerable Man" returned home to the Omaha people.

Organizations and Online Sites

Omaha Tribal Chairman
P.O. Box 368,
Macy, NE 68039-0368

History and Stories of Nebraska: Logan Fontenelle
http://www.ukans.edu/~kansite/hvn/books/nbstory/story23.html
Gives a brief overview of the life of the well-known Omaha tribal chief.

Karl Bodmer
http://monet.unk.edu/mona/artexplr/bodmer/bodmer.html
Features the Swiss artist who visited Omaha territory during the mid-1800s and painted the people and their way of life. Three of Bodmer's paintings are included in this book.

The Omaha Tribe
http://www.omaha.lib.ne.us./transmiss/congress/omaha.html
Describes the physical characteristics, diet, and dress of the Omaha. From this site, click over to the Indian Congress Photo Gallery for images of the Omaha and other tribes.

A Note on Sources

Over a two-year span, many hours were spent searching for sources of information on the Omaha. The fewer the sources, the more time it takes for the search. But the quality of one or two sources can make up for the lack of quantity, as does *The Omaha Tribe*, a definitive study by Alice C. Fletcher and Francis LaFlesche. The official title of the study is the Twenty-seventh Annual Report of the Bureau of American Ethnology to the Secretary of the Smithsonian Institution, 1905-1906, Washington, D.C., Smithsonian Institution Printing Office, 1911. *Upstream People: An Annotated Research Bibliography of the Omaha Tribe* by Michael L. Tate, 1991, aided in the search for material, as did catalog searches at the libraries and resource centers of the American Museum of Natural History and the Smithsonian Museum of the American Indian. Used-book catalogs and stores and my own collection were yet other sources. The Internet offered current information, as did *The*

New York Times and other newspapers (with family members and friends assisting with clippings).

With all of this material collected, read, and annotated, I spent more months internalizing it. Finally one day I came up with a mental blueprint and an all-important first paragraph and could sit down and write, while continuing to search for more information. Not even publication of the book ends that search, for who knows when more facts about the Omaha will be needed in the future?

—Madelyn Klein Anderson

Index

Numbers in *italics* indicate illustrations.

61

About the Author

Madelyn Klein Anderson holds degrees from Hunter College of the City University of New York, New York University, and the Graduate School of Library and Information Science of Pratt Institute in Brooklyn, New York. Before turning to writing full-time, Mrs. Anderson was an army officer, an occupational therapist, a senior editor of books for young people at a major publishing house, and an editorial consultant to the New York City Board of Education. A native New Yorker who has lived in California, Texas, New Mexico, and Alabama, she finally returned to New York, where she lives in the Tribeca section of Manhattan.